D1646350

EARTH'S CHANGING LANDSCAPE

The Growth of Cities

Robert Snedden

FRANKLIN WATTS
LONDON•SYDNEY

This edition 2007

Franklin Watts
338 Euston Road
London NW1 3BH

Franklin Watts Australia
Hachette Children's Books
Level 17/207 Kent Street
Sydney, NSW 2000

Copyright © Franklin Watts 2003

All rights reserved.

Series editor: Sarah Peutrill
Series designer: Simon Borrough
Art director: Jonathan Hair
Picture researcher: Juliet Duff
Series consultant: Steve Watts, FRGS, Principal Lecturer in
Geography Education at the University of Sunderland

A CIP catalogue record for this book is available from the British
Library

ISBN: 978 0 7496 7262 1
Dewey Classification: 307.76

Printed in Malaysia

Picture credits:
Corbis: 8 Nik Wheeler; 10 Hulton-Deutsch Collection; 11 Underwood
& Underwood; 21 Collart Herve/Corbis Sygma; 30 Bob Rowan;
Progressive Image; 32 Steve Terrill. James Davis Travel Photography: 9,
16, 27, 33, 38, 41 and endpapers. Digital Vision: 20, 22, 23. Ecoscene: 13;
25 Vicki Coombs; 26 Rod Smith; 31 Wayne Lawlor; 35 Erik Schaffer; 42
Ian Beames. Eye Ubiquitous: 7 David Peez; 12 Charles Friend; 15 Frank
Leather; 18 (right) P .Maurice; 36 Chris Fairclough; 37 Bridget Tily; 39
Stephen Rafferty; 43 Julia Waterlow Still Pictures: 6 Carlos Guarita; 14
Nigel Dickinson; 17 Hjalte Tim; 18 (left) Ron Giling; 19 Hartmut
Schwarzbach; 24 Andrew Testa; 28 NRSC; 34 Romano Cagnoni.
Topham/Image Works: 29 Michael Siluk. Front Cover: Ecoscene. Every
attempt has been made to clear copyright. Should there be any
inadvertent omission, please apply to the publisher for rectification.

Franklin Watts is a division of Hachette Children's Books.

CONTENTS

The rapid growth of the world's cities has brought about some of the most spectacular changes to the landscape of the Earth. Stretching as far as the eye can see cities are awesome sights, and without them the world would be a very different place.

Evidence from the past

Although they are growing faster now than ever before, cities are not a recent development. In fact, some have existed for thousands of years. In cities such as Athens and Rome the evidence of long ago is preserved among the steel and glass of today. In Delhi, big modern buildings exist alongside narrow streets of tiny old shops.

The Parthenon, a temple built nearly 2,500 years ago, looks over the modern city of Athens, Greece.

Early settlements

Humans first started to build real settlements when farming began around 12,000 years ago. Farming provided a lot more people with food, so while some people tended the crops and animals, others found different things to do.

The inhabitants of these settlements had time to learn new skills. Some made tools for the farmers, others made clothes or cooking pots or built houses. Others became record-keepers, priests, organisers and rulers. This was the start of civilisation. The word comes from the Latin *civitas* from which we also get our word city. Cities and civilisation go together.

Follow it through: settlement growth

People begin farming → There is more food to feed the population → People gather around farms →

Getting bigger From these early settlements, the first cities began to emerge. The settlements that grew were probably ones that had certain key elements: a good location, a steady migration of people, organisation and a good infrastructure (such as roads and sewerage systems).

What is a city? At some point settlements became so large or important that they became cities. Today, the definition of what a city is can be quite vague. Dictionaries might describe a city as 'a place larger than a village or town', or as 'an important centre of population'. How large does a place have to be to be called a city? How important? Most of us have a sense of what we mean by a city but there is no worldwide agreed definition that says this is a city, but that is a town. Loosely we might say a city has a relatively high population (more than 50,000 people) who live in urban conditions, in contrast with the rural life of the open country.

India's capital, the modern city of New Delhi, contrasts with the crowded streets of Old Delhi nearby.

Some people can do other tasks ➤ A settlement is created ➤ Other people are attracted to the settlement ➤ The settlement grows

THE FIRST CITIES

The first cities were built in the Tigris-Euphrates Valley about 6,000 years ago, in what is now Iraq. The first Chinese cities were probably founded around 2,000 years later. Bigger populations meant that cities were more complicated to run than villages so successful growth required organisation and a strong infrastructure.

An archaeological dig at Uruk in present-day Iraq. Cities first grew up in this area because it contains easily-navigable rivers and fertile land.

Take it further
Make a list of all the things you'd expect to find in a city.

◆ Look at the nearest large city to you and see if it has them.
◆ What other things does it have that you did not include?
◆ Compare this with ancient Rome.

Keeping it running Like the cities of today, early cities had public buildings where people could meet and places to store food, weapons and raw materials.

The centre of the city would usually have the ruler's palace and a place of worship. There might be an inner city wall protecting these important places. Houses crowded together around the central area as they do in inner city areas today.

Follow it through: early cities

Cities become larger → Trade routes between settlements are built → People can migrate to cities

Rome and after According to legend, Rome was founded in 753BCE, probably by shepherds and farmers. At the height of the Roman Empire, some 800 years later, Rome was the world's first city of a million people. The Romans had a highly efficient water supply and sewerage system to meet the needs of the people.

All the cities in the Roman Empire saw growth during this period. This was probably made possible by the road network, which was built throughout the Empire and allowed easy access to the cities. After the fall of the Western Roman Empire in 476CE its infrastructure and roads fell into disrepair and with it the importance of cities.

European Medieval cities
From the fall of the Roman Empire until around 1000CE, city populations fell as people moved to the countryside.

At this time some European cities might only have had populations of a few hundred. Paris, one of the largest cities, had around 150,000 people, far less than Ancient Rome at its peak.

Around the city a protective wall kept out undesirables. The very poorest people built shelters around the outside, rather like the shanty towns around some cities today. Even inside the city walls conditions were bad. There was little, or no, sanitation. The people simply threw garbage and other wastes into the streets or piled it up outside the city wall. As a result, disease spread quickly and death rates were high.

The Forum was the centre of government in Ancient Rome.

Worldwide Elsewhere in the world, in Asia, Africa and Central America, cities continued to thrive. For example the city of Guangzhou (Canton) in China in 1000CE had twice the population of Paris.

Guangzhou, in fact, had links with Ancient Rome. Merchants from the Roman Empire travelled to Guangzhou to buy silks, spices and tea. After the fall of the Empire, Guangzhou kept up its contacts with traders in the West. Arab merchants were visiting the city in the seventh century CE. These trade links were vital to the healthy growth of the city.

The city population grows ➤ The city's sanitation cannot cope ➤ Disease spreads quickly and death rates are high ➤ The growing population is stalled

INDUSTRIAL CITIES

Narrow streets of workers' houses leading to the factories, such as this one in Newcastle, UK, were built in industrial towns.

The big change in the development of cities came with the Industrial Revolution. Cities began to grow rapidly, spreading out across the landscape.

Where and when?
Britain was the first country to see the growth of industrial cities in the 18th century. Similar changes followed in other European countries, then in the USA and Japan during the 19th century. In the 20th century Eastern Europe, China, India and south-east Asia became industrialised.

Technology and the urban shift
As industrialisation speeded up, new technology was invented and produced on a grand scale. The machines were made of iron and the power to drive them came from coal. Cities that had developed close to these vital resources, such as Manchester in the UK and Pittsburgh in Pennsylvania, USA, had a huge advantage.

At the same time as technology was making manufacturing more efficient, improvements in agriculture reduced the need for farm workers.

Follow it through: industrialisation

New technology is invented

Factories are established in cities

Fewer farm workers are needed

People once again moved from the country to the city to work in the new factories that were being built. Between 1685 and 1851 the population of Manchester, UK, grew 50 times bigger. After industrialising, Chicago, in the USA, grew from a small town to a population of just over a million in only 50 years.

Chicago's Union Station was built in 1925. Today more than 50,000 commuters pass through it every day.

Communication

The invention of the railways and the building of canals saw trade expand between the industrial cities. Eventually these changes began to spread to all parts of the world, although many countries are not fully industrialised even today.

The working population

The growth of the cities did not bring about better conditions for the people who lived there. The huge machines producing goods quickly and cheaply in the factories did not need the skills of a craft worker to operate. The factory workers were made to work long hours for little pay and they were poorly housed. As they had no means other than walking to get to work, their homes were built

Take it further
Choose a large city.

◆ Find out how much the population has grown over the past 100 years, perhaps using the Internet. Look at www.citypopulation.de.
◆ Find out how the city has grown – is it mainly through immigration or increasing birthrates?

near the factory. In fact, transport, or the lack of it, was one of the major factors shaping the growth of the cities. We can still see workers' homes in the narrow streets of today's inner cities.

Public transport and the suburbs

The wealthy owners of the factories had no need to live close to their noisy and polluting workplaces. They could afford to build big houses on the outskirts of the city and travel by carriage. So too could the bankers who financed them and the merchants who sold the goods the factories made.

By the 1800s, however, as public transport systems became established, living on the outskirts of the city came within the means of the less well off. People could now move from the crowded inner city to the greater comfort of the suburbs.

People move to the cities for work ▶ Cities grow ▶ Better transport and infrastructure in cities is needed

WE'LL BUILD IT HERE

When the first settlements were being built there was no shortage of sites to choose from. So what did the settlers look for when they decided where to build?

Down by the riverside One of the most important considerations is a supply of food and fresh water. This makes a site by a river a good choice. The river provides water to irrigate crops, it can be a source of fish to supplement the diet, and it provides a line of defence, as any attackers will have to cross the river first. The floodplains around the river are also likely to have rich fertile soils from the sediment carried down by the river.

The city of Venice in Italy is situated on more than 100 islands in a lagoon off the Adriatic Sea. Before about 450CE the islands had a small native population of simple, poor fishermen. Now Venice has grown to a population of over 85,000 and is an important tourist centre.

Follow it through: city sites

Early settlers choose a site

Population increases

Fertile land Several important early settlements grew up in river valleys. The earliest of all cities grew up in the Tigris-Euphrates Valley in present-day Iraq. Silt deposited by the rivers made this one of the most fertile areas. River flooding is controlled by dykes and canals carry the water to the fields.

Other river valleys, such as the Nile Valley in Egypt, the Huang Ho (Yellow River) Valley in China and the Indus Valley of India and Pakistan, were the starting points of some of the world's greatest cities.

On a hill Building on a hill also provided the settlement with some protection. The ancient cities of Athens and Rome are examples of this strategy. If the settlement was attacked, the defenders had the advantage of fighting from high ground.

Trade Although it may not have been of great importance in deciding where to build initially, the opportunity to trade with other settlements plays a big part in deciding which settlements will grow and thrive.

Coastal settlements had the ready advantage of the sea. Ships could carry people and trade goods from one settlement to another along the coast and to those further inland that were built on navigable rivers. Cities such as London, Venice, Chicago and Hong Kong all owe much of their success to their position by the waterways.

The city of Hong Kong has become one of the world's major centres for trade.

Take it further
The site is the location where the settlement was first built. The situation is how that location relates to other settlements and the surrounding landscape. So site determines where a settlement is founded, and situation determines whether or not that settlement will grow.

◆ Look at a map of a city and work out why its situation is good.

The water supply is not large enough	People move away	Settlement fails
The water supply is okay	Trade with other cities	City grows

Some cities seem to have been built in places that are far from ideal. The runaway growth of the cities in the developing world has seen vast concentrations of people in what are potentially some of the most hazardous places in the world. In 1950, around 50 million people were affected in one way or another by natural disasters: by 2000 that number had climbed to over 250 million.

A relief camp in the Philippines where hundreds of thousands of refugees were forced to live after the eruption of Mount Pinatubo.

Cities near volcanoes Cities have developed near volcanoes because volcanic soils are some of the richest in the world, making them ideal for farming. Volcanic lava is also often rich in valuable minerals such as gold, copper and zinc. These things would have made the area attractive to early settlers. As volcanoes often stay dormant for hundreds or thousands of years, settlements can become well established between eruptions. Even the threat of an eruption may not be enough to check the growth of the city.

On 9 June 1991, Mount Pinatubo, a volcano north of Manila, capital of the Philippines, erupted. Over 700 people were killed and 200,000 buildings were destroyed. On 19 December 2000, Popocatepetl, a volcano close to Mexico City and its 18 million inhabitants, erupted. Nearby valleys were filled with lava and 30,000 people had to be evacuated.

Earthquakes

Some 40 of the world's 50 fastest growing cities are in earthquake zones. Many cities have grown up in areas where earthquakes are relatively frequent.

But why are cities built in earthquake zones? For one thing it is difficult to tell you are in an earthquake zone until one actually happens. By the time the settlers have realised they are in the wrong place there may be nowhere else to go, or rebuilding is preferable to evacuation.

Over 120,000 buildings collapsed or were damaged by the Kobe earthquake in Japan.

Economic development

Response to earthquakes is likely to be better organised in more economically developed countries (MEDCs) than in in less economically developed countries (LEDCs). The buildings are also more able to withstand the tremor.

On 17 January 1995 a powerful earthquake struck the city of Kobe in Japan, a MEDC. Around 5,000 people died and hundreds of thousands were made homeless as highways and buildings collapsed. In contrast, an earthquake that hit part of Turkey, a LEDC, in 1999 killed more than three times as many people, even though it was less powerful than the Kobe earthquake.

Mega-disasters

96 per cent of the deaths resulting from natural disasters take place in LEDCs. Some people think it only a matter of time before the first 'mega-disaster' affecting over a million people strikes an LEDC city. This might be flooding in Dhaka in Bangladesh or an earthquake devastating Mexico City.

Case study: San Fransisco, USA

An earthquake may be only the beginning of the problems for the city it hits.

1906
In 1906 the city of San Francisco was hit by a powerful earthquake that took 500 lives and destroyed 1.2 square kilometres in the centre of the city. In addition to the damage caused by the quake itself, broken power lines and fractured gas pipes resulted in the outbreak of terrible fires that took three days to control. The earthquake, however, brought about the renewal of the city. It was rebuilt with better buildings and design. By 1915 all traces of the disaster had gone.

1989
San Francisco was struck again in 1989. A ten-metre section of the San Francisco-Oakland Bay Bridge collapsed and 1,400 homes were destroyed. But this time only 68 people died.

The future
San Fransisco is likely to be struck by earthquakes in the future, but the city continues to grow despite this prospect.

THE GROWING CITY

As more people migrate to a city there is pressure on it to grow. Ancient cities, originally built to house a few thousand people and surrounded by defensive walls, had to expand to accommodate people seeking a better way of life. Some of this growth was thought out by planners and some has happened haphazardly.

Work started on the redevelopment of Canary Wharf in London's Dockland area in 1988.

Tear down the walls? Many ancient cities were surrounded by walls that gave protection against enemies and controlled the passage of goods in and out of the city. But the walls not only kept people outside from coming in, but also stopped the people inside from building out.

City buildings had to be built taller and closer together, which added to the feeling of overcrowding. Some cities solved the space problem, temporarily at least, by knocking the walls down and rebuilding them further out. Others built outside the walls, leaving the old walled city at the heart of the new expanded city, or just knocked their walls down altogether.

Still growing As these older cities – such as Rome and London – are still growing today, they continue to face decisions about where to grow. The oldest parts of such cities, including old city walls and buildings, are often protected. In London the neglected Docklands area to the east of the city was chosen for major business and housing development in the late 1980s.

Follow it through: city walls

Settlements become richer

They build walls for protection

In the heart of the city

Today we call the area of the city where most businesses are based, the central business district (CBD). For many cities this was where the original settlement had its beginnings. The city's transport system will have its focus on this area, as its aim will be to bring large numbers of people into and out of the business district every day. Mainline railway stations will be in or near the CBD.

Space still limited

Similarly to the old city wall problem, the space in the CBD is limited. Planners today solve this by expanding upwards rather than outwards and so we see the city's tallest buildings here. Sydney, the largest city in Australia, saw rapid development in the 1960s, with a spectacular new skyline of high-rise office blocks that replaced older buildings in the downtown area and along its harbour.

The inner city

The inner city is the area that immediately borders the CBD. This is likely to be one of the oldest parts of the city and may suffer from decay and neglect. As it is sandwiched between the CBD and outer city developments there is likely to be great pressure on land use in the inner city as there is nowhere for it to grow into. There may be long streets of terraced houses laid out in grid-like patterns. There will be few green spaces and the streets are often congested, as there are no spaces for off-street parking.

Many tall buildings rise up in the downtown district of Sydney, Australia, an important centre of business and finance.

Secure within the walls, city culture develops

The city outgrows its walls

The walls may be left behind, a relic of the past in the city centre

THE URBAN SHIFT

In the year 2000, more than 76 per cent of people in MEDCs lived in cities. In contrast, in LEDCs the proportion was only 40 per cent, but by 2030 it is predicted that over half the people of the developing world will be living in cities. There are two reasons why city populations are growing. The birth rate naturally increases the population, and people move into the cities from outside.

Every year many people move from rural areas to Kenya's capital city, Nairobi.

Pulled to the city What are the factors that make people decide to move to the city? They can be divided into two groups – push factors and pull factors.

People living in rural areas can be 'pulled' to the city by the belief that they will improve their standard of living through better-paid jobs, or simply having the opportunity to find work. They may believe that their children will get a better education in the city and that health care will be easier to come by. For people in the MEDCs, the bright lights and excitement of city life might be enough of a pull to make them relocate.

Pushed from the country People in the LEDCs may also be 'pushed' from their rural homes to the urban environment by pressures caused by increasing population and the demands it makes on resources in the rural areas. Drought and crop failure may force a migration towards the city.

Three-quarters of Kenya's people, such as these Masai, still live in rural areas. About 40 per cent of Kenyan farmers live in poverty conditions, forcing some to migrate to a city.

Follow it through: the urban shift

Health care in cities tends to be better

People move to the city to find a better life

Shanty towns The speed at which the urban population is growing in the LEDCs is causing many problems. Many of the people end up living in poor and overcrowded shanty towns on the outskirts of the cities. Because they cannot afford to live elsewhere they have to build their own accommodation using scrap materials. Basic services such as clean water and sanitation may be scarce or lacking altogether.

Take it further
City populations grow for two reasons: an increased birth rate and migration.

◆ Choose two cities, one in an MEDC and one in an LEDC.
◆ Compare their population growth over the last ten years. Try to find out how much of it is due to each factor.

Natural growth As well as growth from migration, city populations, particularly in LEDCs, are being swollen by natural increases as the birth rate exceeds the death rate. Outside the shanty towns, hygiene and medical care tend, on the whole, to be better in the cities than in the rural areas. This means that the death rate is lowered so the city population grows faster. But this growing population puts pressure on the cities' infrastructures.

Many of the people who move from the country to the city find themselves living in slum conditions rather than finding a better way of life.

The city is overcrowded

Some people live in shanty towns

Quality of life is similar or poorer than in the country

INFRASTRUCTURE

A healthy city needs to be looked after. It requires an infrastructure – public facilities and services such as schools, fire and police stations, roads and transportation systems, and water and sewerage systems. The quality of life for the inhabitants of the city will depend on how well the city government maintains its infrastructure.

Accessible services Providing access to the services that meet people's needs in the city is an important part of city planning. Those people living in the wealthier parts of a city will often have the best services and, because they are likely to be car owners, they will have the easiest access to them. Poorer citizens will have to make do with the services that are close by.

Mexico City is one of the world's largest cities and has seen rapid growth in its population. With a poor public transport infrastructure, vehicle ownership has increased. Exhaust fumes from motor vehicles combine with dust from unpaved streets and with industrial smoke, leading to highly-polluted air becoming trapped over the city. This is called photochemical smog.

Water use

The development of urban life-styles has brought about great increases in water use. In the USA, for example, daily water use averages about 7,200 litres per person. This includes 500 litres for domestic uses, 3,000 litres for irrigation, and 3,700 litres for industry. Water treatment and distribution systems have to match the increased demand.

Struggling to keep up

The rapid growth in the population of many cities in LEDCs has left the authorities facing a huge task to provide adequate services. In cities such as Rio de Janeiro, Mexico City and Calcutta, city infrastructures are pushed to the limit.

Running water and proper sewerage, provisions that city-dwellers in the MEDCs take for granted, are often only available in certain areas of LEDC cities. The drinking water may be contaminated, and uncollected rubbish provides another opportunity for disease to take hold.

Case study: Dhaka, Bangladesh

The population of Dhaka has increased enormously in recent decades, until it is now one of the largest Asian cities with a population of about 10 million, up from 3.5 million in 1951.

Infrastructure strain

This has put severe strain on the city's infrastructure, and the city now suffers from increased air pollution and congestion, water pollution from industries discharging waste into rivers, a poor drainage system, and a waste collection and disposal system that can only serve 15 to 20 per cent of the city population.

The future

Plans drawn up to tackle the problem require a great deal of money and time. And they do not include the fifth of the population that live in the city's slums.

A water collection facility in Manaus, Brazil. As more people go to live in the city extra standpipes are set up, but many people, including children, have to go far to access clean water.

A landfill site. The landfill process involves daily spreading and compacting of waste into a layer. This is covered by soil to seal it from rodents and insects and to cover unpleasant smells from the decaying waste.

One of the most important roles of a city's infrastructure is to deal with the huge amounts of waste produced by a lot of people living together.

Waste disposal in MEDCs

In most modern MEDCs waste is disposed of in one of two ways: it is removed from the city and buried in landfill sites, or it is incinerated.

Landfill sites are usually outside the city. Various sites are used, from abandoned quarries to marshy areas. Sometimes they can cause dramatic changes to the landscape such as the creation of new hills. A covered and landscaped hill of waste can solve a waste-disposal problem and actually improve the environment. Landfilling can also allow land to be used for other purposes that were not possible before. So, the city influences the landscape outside its perimeter.

As city populations grow, the search for suitable landfill sites becomes more difficult. Residential suburbs, surrounding some cities, are often hostile to landfill sites because of the pollution they cause, and conflict arises.

Follow it through: landfill sites

Waste is buried in a landfill site

Landfill site eventually becomes full

Case study: waste management in New York City, USA

A city like New York has to shift well over 30,000 tonnes of rubbish every single day.

Landfill sites

For more than 50 years, until 2001, half of New York's waste was carried by barge to the Fresh Kills landfill site, south of the city on Staten Island. Since then the city of New York has been working to reduce waste and encourage recycling, including building a paper-recycling mill on Staten Island. Even so, New York cannot deal with all of the waste it generates. The city exports millions of tonnes of waste every year to landfills in other states, such as Pennsylvania and Virginia.

Take it further

Find out how much of your daily rubbish can be recycled.

◆ What processes does it go through?
◆ What percentage of your region's rubbish is recycled?
◆ Think of some ways to encourage more people to recycle their rubbish.

A woman searches through an open waste site in Manila in the Philippines.

Waste disposal in LEDCs In some LEDCs waste is not as efficiently processed. In the slum areas and shanty towns around the major cities basic amenities may be entirely absent. In fast-growing cities, such as Sao Paulo, Brazil, rubbish is left to rot in the streets. In many places people search through rubbish and take it back home for the family to sort through and recycle as much as they can.

Landfill site re-landscaped

New sites need to be found

Local residents object to new landfill sites

Cities have to find alternatives for disposing of rubbish

KEEPING THINGS MOVING

One of the biggest problems for city planners is traffic congestion: too many cars and other vehicles all trying to squeeze into a relatively small area at the same time.

The problem with older cities
As the CBD often develops in the oldest part of a city the streets are sometimes narrow, and not at all suited to modern traffic levels. Most traffic congestion is related to people commuting to and from work. The pressures on the road and railway systems leading into the city centre can be immense at the beginning and end of the working day.

At the same time all those vehicles contribute to air and noise pollution, making the city an unpleasant environment in which to live and work.

Public transport solution?
Cities, therefore, either have to change their structure so that the businesses are not all located in one place, or they have to find better ways to get people into the CBD. Better public transport systems, such as buses, trains and trams are one way. But however bad the traffic, many people prefer the convenience of their own cars.

Travelling by train in Calcutta, India. Trains here may be a convenient form of transport but they can become over-crowded.

Follow it through: traffic reduction

Centre of cities are congested

Parking restrictions or congestion charging introduced

Case study: congestion charging in London, UK

London is one of the world's busiest cities. Traffic congestion can be so bad that drivers spend half their time queuing and not actually getting anywhere. In 2003 the Mayor of London introduced a scheme of congestion charging.

Daily toll

Private motorists pay a fee to bring their cars into central London. This has led to a 20 per cent fall in traffic within the charge zone. The money raised from the scheme is ploughed back into the public transport system. However, city centre shops and small businesses have complained that their trade has suffered as a result of fewer customers.

Keeping the traffic moving in city centres is a problem for planners. One solution tried in London is to charge motorists who bring their cars into the city.

Take it further

Traffic levels are on the increase in China's capital, Beijing. The number of cars on the city streets is increasing by around 10 per cent every year as more people are able to afford cars. See the box below for the various proposed solutions to deal with the problem.

◆ Can you think of any more ways to combat congestion?
◆ Which method do you think might be the most effective?

Proposed solutions to Beijing's congestion crisis:

1 Increase parking fees – car owners are among the highest paid people, so this might not deter many.

2 Add more roads, running alongside existing ones – experience has shown that if roads are made wider more people use them, so the congestion is not eased. Alternative routes might bring some relief.

3 Add more stations to the subway system – at present stations on the Beijing subway are often far apart. Adding more might encourage subway use as people would be able to reach their destinations more easily.

More people shop at out-of-town supermarkets

Traffic moves better

Small businesses have less trade

City centre declines

THE WIDER IMPACT

The growth of a city not only impacts on the city itself but also on the landscape and other settlements near and far. Cities are hungry for resources. The larger they grow the more their demands for energy and materials increase.

Raw materials The millions of people living and working in the city all need to be supplied with food and drink; they need places to work; and they need places to live, to shop and to be entertained. The sheer volume of raw materials required to supply this demand is huge.

Built around the city If you look at a road map you'll notice that major roads all lead into cities. Often a country's whole infrastructure is centred on its major cities. You'll also notice that usually roads take the most direct route between settlements. To do this requires natural landscapes to be altered, for example the removal of forests and cuttings through high ground.

Major routes into a city are often heavy with traffic feeding the city's need for resources.

Follow it through: city footprints

Cities need lots of resources

They cannot produce everything they need

These tea-pickers in Sri Lanka will probably never see any of the cities where their tea will be drunk.

From far away A city does not just affect its immediate surroundings. The demands of large populations can also affect landscapes thousands of kilometres away. Indeed, a large city affects the global environment. For example, consider the tea that goes to Paris from India, the copper for pipes that might come from mines in Zambia, the timber from forests in Scandinavia. People living in rural environments may find that their economic survival depends on being able to satisfy the demands of cities on the other side of the globe.

In addition there is the environmental cost of shipping food and other materials into the cities. Flying fruit from distant countries around the world can use up a hundred times more energy than the fruit itself contains.

Case study: Vancouver, Canada
We all have an impact on the environment because we all use natural resources in one way or another. Environmentalists call the mark we make on nature our 'ecological footprint'.

Huge demands
Cities have giant footprints. It has been calculated that Vancouver actually needs an area of the Earth that is 174 times bigger than the city itself to supply its needs. Cities have been described as 'black holes' sucking up the ecological output of entire regions.

Resources taken from all over the world

Cities affect the Earth's landscape even far away

THE SUBURBS

As city centre areas grew polluted and crowded, some people began to move out towards the edge of the city. The growth of the areas around a city, as residential and commercial sectors spring up, is called suburbanisation.

Moving out The movement of people to the suburbs accelerated through the second half of the 20th century as public transport systems were improved and as more people were able to afford cars.

Life in the suburbs looks very attractive to many people. In the suburbs housing is likely to be larger and of better quality than in the inner city areas. It is more spread out as pressures on land use are not so great as they are in the city centre.

An aerial view of suburban homes with swimming pools in California, USA. Seen from above suburbs often make a regular pattern across the landscape, created by the uniformity of the housing.

Follow it through: suburbanisation

City centres become crowded

City expands outwards to cope

'Mall of America', Minnesota, the largest shopping complex in the USA. Shopping centres are getting increasingly larger, and can become almost like small towns in themselves.

Commuting
Many of the people who live in the suburbs are likely to find employment in the city rather than locally, although increasingly high-tech industries may relocate to suburban locations.

Shopping
Suburban residents may use centralised shopping centres, or malls, rather than traditional 'high streets' or local shops.

Boomburbs
Suburban cities, a hybrid of the suburb and the city, are now becoming 'boomburbs'. They look like suburbs but enough people live there for them to rank as cities in their own right. There are over 50 boomburbs in the USA. Each has a population of at least 100,000 people and they have all shown a rapid rate of growth. Four of the boomburbs have populations that exceed 300,000, making them bigger than Miami in the USA.

These boomburbs are vast sprawling cities, but they do not have a central business district as other similar-sized cities. Shopping, entertainment and offices are spread out rather than being concentrated in one place.

Richer people move to the suburbs

Inner city becomes run-down

The ring of suburbs forms an outer city around the original city centre

Small communities on the outskirts of a city can be transformed to meet the city's needs. They become overspill towns, providing housing for city workers but, like boomburbs, they may even become cities in their own right. Other 'new towns' may be built from scratch on carefully selected sites.

Satellite towns Towns that form naturally around cities, created by their overspill, are called satellite towns. They appear to be independent, but are usually dependent on the neighbouring city, for example for jobs.

When the new capital of Brazil, Brasília, was being built at the end of the 1950s, the huge number of workers involved were housed in construction camps. As work progressed on the city most of the construction camps were torn down. Some of the residents moved into shanty towns, which grew into the satellite towns of Brasília.

The Brazilian satellite town inhabitants considered the growing shanty towns to be more desirable places to live than the rigidly planned environment of Brasília.

Over 75,000 people live in the edge city of Schaumburg, Illinois, but it still calls itself a village!

Edge cities In the USA edge cities have developed in areas close to the major roads that lead to older cities like Los Angeles and Washington, DC. Thirty years earlier no one would have guessed a city would appear in such places. First shopping malls appear in the suburbs so people don't have to travel to the city to shop. Then jobs move out as well so people don't have to travel into the major city to work. Eventually all the facilities people need, including entertainment and recreation facilities, are also in place.

Follow it through: edge cities

Cities are linked by major roads

People live by the roads as they provide easy access to the city

New towns When cities can no longer support the population, deliberately planning 'new towns', rather than haphazardly building outwards, is sometimes the solution.

The decades after the Second World War saw the building of such new towns in the UK. These were designed to take the overspill from the cities by providing homes for the urban workforce and alternative locations for businesses outside the city. They were to be self-supporting communities in their own right. Today, over two million people live in more than 30 new towns around the UK.

In Singapore, older properties around the central business district were cleared for redevelopment and people were instead housed in purpose built satellite towns. Each new town holds about 250,000 people, all living within 12 kilometres of the CBD.

Because there is such pressure on land use, many people in Singapore live in modern high-rise developments in satellite towns.

Shops are built for convenience

Jobs move out of the city

The area grows and eventually becomes an edge city

KEEP IT GREEN

Expanding cities put increasing pressure on the landscape around them. As cities expand outwards they swallow up undeveloped land and towns and villages, which are transformed into suburbs. The boundaries between rural and urban environments can become blurred, with one gradually blending into the other.

Urban sprawl

The development of residential and industrial centres on undeveloped land at the edge of the city is called 'urban sprawl'. Rural land values are less than city land values and it is easier to build on a rural site, rather than clearing and redeveloping a city centre site.

However, it is often recognised that green areas around the cities are part of the landscape that should not be developed. In the USA, for example, 70 per cent of farmland is located around urban areas and may one day be swallowed by cities. In the 1990s around 1.5 million hectares of open land (including farmland and forests) were developed.

Consequences

But urban sprawl has wider consequences. Wetland areas are natural sponges for rain and if they are removed some areas are more at risk from flooding. Whole ecosystems are also threatened, affecting both animals and plants.

Portland in Oregon is protected by an urban growth boundary.

Case study: Oregon, USA

Each of the cities in Oregon is surrounded by an urban growth boundary, beyond which growth is restricted. Land outside the boundary will remain rural, and even urban developments like sewers are restricted.

Results

These urban growth boundaries have been highly effective. They have saved farmland from urban sprawl and have led to better co-ordination of planning.

Follow it through: urban sprawl

People are concerned about urban sprawl

Growth of cities is restricted

Green areas are maintained

Managing urban sprawl

There are several ways to check the growth of cities into green areas. In the US anti-sprawl intitiatives have been introduced in some states. Methods include farm protection, planned and managed growth away from natural wildlife, and transport planning – extra roads can increase sprawl.

In the UK, planners impose a similar limit on a city's growth – a surrounding area called the 'green belt' that cannot be used for housing.

Such initiatives have lots of positive effects. It forces planners to make the most of the space available inside the inner city area – redeveloping run-down urban areas for example. However, it can put pressure on the prices of the available urban housing. When rent and house prices rise, lower-paid workers can no longer afford to live in the city.

Take It further

Look at a map of a city near you. How many green areas, such as parks, can you see?

◆ Are they well-spaced out?
◆ If you were planning the city would you want to make any changes to the green areas?

Green cities

As well as keeping the countryside around the city green, it is important to have green spaces within the city as well. People with access to parks and gardens are generally happier and healthier.

Many city planners turn wasteland into green areas and urban farms, and disused railway lines into safe cycle routes through the city. As well as improving the city, this relieves pressure on the outskirts.

Golden Gate Park in San Francisco is one of the largest city parks in the USA.

re people want to e in the city

House prices are pushed up

Some people cannot afford to live in the city

WHERE SHALL WE LIVE?

City populations are dynamic. People tend not to live in the same places all their lives. They move to and from different areas of the city or out of the city altogether. Others move into the city from other cities or rural areas.

In Bergen, Norway, the old part of the town is built totally out of wood.

Affordable housing Which parts of the city do people choose to live in? The short answer may be that they live where they can afford to. City centres are where land values are highest. Banks, offices and large retailers can afford these prices, but ordinary residents cannot.

The older housing in the city will be found in the inner city areas bordering the CBD. Here land values are often lower, so this may be where many of the city's poorest residents are found. Further out, where the suburbs begin, a wide range of homes cater to the varying needs of the middle-income and higher-income earners.

Follow it through: counter-urbanisation

People live where they can afford to

Higher-income families move out of the run-down inner city

Lower-income groups move in

34

Filtering As the housing stock in the inner city deteriorates with age, or becomes less desirable as its position within the city changes when the city expands, higher-income groups may move out and lower-income groups move in.

The process by which social groups move from one part of a city to another is called filtering. Another example of filtering is given on page 39.

Another example of filtering is given on page 39.

Take it further

Conduct a survey of how people decide where they will live.

◆ Interview at least ten people.
◆ Think of five questions to ask to find out what is important to them. You could think up a rating scale such as 1 = not important; 5 = very important.
◆ Put your responses into a chart or table.

In many parts of Singapore ramshackle older housing can still be seen next to the modern apartment buildings.

Counter-urbanisation

In the last part of the 20th century the process of urbanisation began to be reversed in many of the cities of the MEDCs. City populations began to decline in London, Chicago and Paris among others, as people moved out of the cities. In a process called counter-urbanisation, people moved to villages and towns that were still within reach of the city but which offered what was seen as a better quality of life.

This has an inevitable effect on the life and landscape in the villages. The demand for a limited number of houses pushes prices up beyond the means of the rural population. Cheaper housing estates may be built around the village and the character of the village that had made it so appealing in the first place may be lost. Such movements of people mean that many towns and cities are constantly changing – they may move from being undesirable to desirable and back again.

Centre of the city becomes further run-down ▶ More people move out ▶ City population falls

Different ethnic communities are often a characteristic of cities. People move to cities of other countries for similar reasons that attract most people to cities: better jobs, life-styles and standard of living.

Large cities, such as New York, are 'melting pots' where people of many cultures and backgrounds live and work.

Living apart Although people of different ethnic backgrounds might work together, they tend to live apart. The reasons for this may be a feeling of security and the opportunity to preserve their culture and language. In the USA, Black, Asian and Hispanic populations are most likely to be found in city centre areas. By contrast, over half of all non-Hispanic white Americans live in the suburbs. In the UK, similarly, different ethnic populations live in separate city areas.

Influencing an area This coming together of an immigrant community in one place can have a great effect on an area. They may open special shops and build new religious buildings. In time the type of housing they prefer will determine the housing that is built in that area.

Chinatown Many cities, including Sydney, Montreal, London and New York, have an area that Chinese immigrants have made their own. The Chinatown area of a city can be one of its most colourful and vibrant places. It gives people an opportunity to sample the culture and tradition of another country, practically on their doorstep.

The Chinatown areas of major cities, such as this one in Sydney, Australia, provide all that the Chinese population might need.

City contrasts While immigrants may thrive in many cities, some experience poverty. The difference in the quality of housing available to wealthy people compared to poor people can be immense. Immigrants drawn to city life can often find themselves struggling to find adequate housing. The response in some cities is to build cheap multi-story housing, which many feel ruins the city landscape.

Case study: Sydney, Australia

Urban development in Sydney is a hot issue because the city's growth is limited by national parks to the north and south and the Blue Mountains to the west. As land becomes scarcer, urban development onto agricultural land is a concern.

Immigration

Immigrants are attracted to Sydney because it is a dynamic city and because they can find people from the same country or ethnicity there. Once in the city, immigrants frequently settle in areas where people speak a language they know, where there are churches, temples or mosques, cultural associations, community workers to help them, and the food they are familiar with.

Planning dilemma

The fact that immigrants make up 75 per cent of Sydney's annual population growth makes planning difficult. Immigration increases the demand for housing, drives up prices and strains the city's infrastructure. But if planners concentrate on improving the immigrant areas it will lead to neglect of the areas lived in by other communities.

REGENERATE, REDEVELOP, REVIVE

The process of counter-urbanisation, and the problems of poor housing may be reversed if the city properties are renovated and the area is regenerated.

This modern architecture in Lisbon, Portugal is a striking contrast to some of the city's older buildings.

Reurbanisation Some cities in MEDCs have begun a process of redeveloping their inner city areas with a view to attracting businesses and people back to the city. This may include clearing slum properties, building new transport systems, erecting modern buildings, shopping areas and leisure facilities and setting up small-scale developments of high-tech industry to replace old-style manufacturing industries.

In Denmark, for example, selected areas have been regenerated to improve worn-down buildings, increase leisure facilities and decrease traffic.

Follow it through: urban regeneration Older properties in the city centre decay with age and neglect The city centre becomes an unpleasant place to be

Brownfield sites Sites within cities that are cleared and redeveloped in this way are called brownfield sites. Sites that have never been built on are called greenfield sites. Often greenfield sites are protected so that they cannot be developed, which is why brownfield sites can provide a good alternative.

Newly-built apartments built on the brownfield site of a former engineering works.

Take it further
Find out more about the European City of Culture scheme.

◆ Which city is City of Culture now?
◆ What has the city done to improve itself since its nomination?

Cultural regeneration

Cultural regeneration can also occur when the city focuses on its heritage to make itself more attractive to cash-generating tourists and to those seeking a site for new business ventures.

The European Union finances a European City of Culture initiative. Each year a city is chosen and receives a subsidy from the European Commission. The additional visitors drawn to the city bring a welcome boost to its funds.

Gentrification
Another relatively new process is gentrification, where middle-income homeowners move into and upgrade inner city properties. The attractions of the inner city for professionals is that they are close to their place of work in the CBD, they have easy access to the amenities and entertainment also found there and, initially at least, housing is cheaper.

As the first wave of people improve their properties the area becomes more desirable to others. The original lower-income inhabitants find themselves being priced out as more middle- and higher-income earners move in and so the social composition of the area is changed. This is part of the filtering process (see page 35).

Time and money is invested in regenerating the city centre

More people and businesses are drawn back

The city begins to thrive again

WHERE WILL IT END?

Is there any limit to how big cities can become? Where does a city end? As we have seen, some cities have their growth restricted by planners but there may be no such restriction for other cities.

Megacities
In 1925, only London, New York and Berlin had populations of over three million. By the beginning of the 21st century, the world's ten biggest cities all had more than ten million people. London doesn't even make the top ten list anymore. The biggest city in the world today is Tokyo, followed by Mexico City, Mumbai (Bombay) and Sao Paulo. By 2015 it is estimated that there will be more than 20 cities with over 10 million people, and all but four will be in LEDCs.

Megalopolis
In 1961, French geographer Jean Gottmann used the word 'megalopolis' to describe the sprawling urban area of the north-eastern United States that stretched over 700 kilometres from Boston in the north to Baltimore and Washington, DC, in the south. Today, the BosWash megalopolis covers 130,000 square kilometres and has a total population of some 44 million people, or about 16 per cent of the population of the USA.

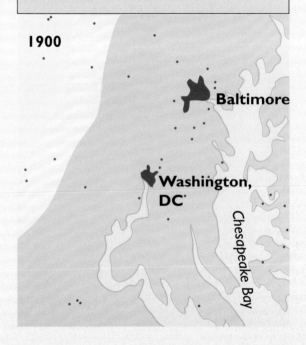

The development of the cities of Washington, DC, and Baltimore over the past 100 years. The red shows the growth of urban areas.

1900

Baltimore

Washington, DC

Chesapeake Bay

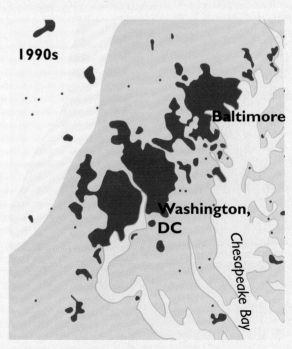

1990s

Baltimore

Washington, DC

Chesapeake Bay

Follow it through: megalopolis creation

The world population increases all the time

Eventually, most people will live in cities

A sprawling mixture Gottmann said that cities are no longer single units, separate from their rural and urban neighbours. Cities spread out into the countryside that surrounds them, becoming a mix of urban, suburban and rural landscapes.

Other megalopolises are developing in the US, from Chicago to Pittsburgh and along the coast of California from San Francisco Bay to San Diego.

Elsewhere in the world the Tokyo-Yokohama-Osaka area forms an example of a megalopolis in Japan. The Tokyo metropolitan area alone is one of the most densely populated areas in the world with a population of over 28 million crammed together, resulting in a density of about 14,000 people in every square kilometre.

The city of Tokyo, Japan, is one of the most crowded places on the planet.

The cities grow larger

The boundaries between cities become blurred

It becomes harder to distinguish rural from urban landscapes

People thronging the streets of Delhi. The explosive growth in city populations puts a huge strain on resources.

We have seen that already half the world's population lives in cities. By the middle of this century there are likely to be nine billion people in the world – can we possibly build more cities to house them all or expand existing cities sufficiently?

Population growth By 2025, according to some estimates, 65 per cent of the world's population will be city-dwellers. Every year the world's population increases by around 75 million people. 60 million of those people will end up living in cities, most of them in LEDCs.

The rapid growth of cities, particularly in LEDCs, causes many problems. The sheer size of the population in these cities threatens to overwhelm their resources. The infrastructure of the cities is not able to cope with the demands being placed on it. Already many live in grinding poverty in shanty towns. Some estimates suggest that over 600 million people in LEDC cities cannot fulfil their basic needs for water, food, shelter and health.

Follow it through: sustainability

Cities expand too quickly

There are not enough resources for everyone

The lure of the city   Despite all this, people keep being drawn towards the cities. As bad as life may seem there, urban poverty seems preferable to rural poverty. There is a danger that having so many disaffected people crammed together in one place could lead to riots and civil unrest. This is an issue that will have to be faced up to in the near future if all cities are not managed sustainably.

What is sustainability?   Sustainability can be approached from three directions: environmental, social and economic. One definition of sustainability is that the needs of the present generation are met without in any way compromising the ability of future generations to meet their needs. Environmental sustainability means doing no damage to the environment that puts future generations at risk. Social sustainability avoids giving short-term benefits to the few at the expense of long-term benefits for the many. Economic sustainability means improving the economy so that people will be better off in the future and not just today. Norway (see case study) is one country that is attempting to ensure sustainability in its cities.

Case study. Norway

In the 1990s the Sustainable Cities Programme in Norway set out to achieve the objective of making five cities more environmentally friendly.

Sustainable solutions

The main recommendations for the five cities were:

◆ Make public transport the cities' backbone
◆ Maintain and promote green areas
◆ Regenerate streets, squares and parks
◆ Reduce road traffic and develop a complete network of cycle tracks
◆ Ensure that urban design is in keeping with the existing character of the cities
◆ Involve local communities in city planning
◆ Ensure urban housing is healthy, practical, attractive and takes place within existing building areas.

The five cities have now begun the process of implementing these ideas.

Building construction site, China. You don't have to look too far in a city to find evidence of the building and rebuilding that is constantly going on.

People living in cities, especially in LEDCs, suffer from poverty

Sustainable solutions have to be found

GLOSSARY

Amenities   The useful and desirable features of a city, such as shops, cinemas, libraries and so on.

Boomburbs   Rapidly growing suburbs that have become cities in their own right.

Brownfield site   A site for redeveloping in a city that has previously been built on.

CBD   The central business district. An area in the centre of a city where the offices of major businesses, large department stores and so on are located.

Communication   In a country this means the ways by which people and goods are moved, in other words, road, rail and air networks.

Commuters   People who travel some distance between their homes and their place of work each day.

Congestion   Over-crowding of streets in a city so that it becomes difficult for traffic to move.

Counter-urbanisation   The movement of people out of the cities to live in a more rural environment.

Downtown   Another name for the central business district in a city.

Edge cities   New cities that have grown up alongside major roads into existing cities.

Filtering   The movement of people in different social groups from one part of a city to another.

Gentrification   The process of renovating and improving a district in a city to make it appeal to higher-income earners.

Greenfield site   A site that has not been previously built on.

Industrial Revolution   Period of history that began in the middle of the 18th century when production moved from a rural to an urban base.

Infrastructure   The physical and organisational services and facilities needed to run a city properly.

Inner city   The area of a city around the central business district, often where the housing for factory workers was built.

LEDC   Less economically developed country. A country that is not fully industrialised and most of its workforce work in agriculture.

MEDC   More economically developed country. A country that is fully industrialised.

Megalopolis   Name given to a large area where the boundaries of one or more cities have grown together.

New town   A planned town built in a previously undeveloped area.

Sanitation   Facilities to remove sewage and rubbish from buildings.

Satellite town   A small town that is dependent on a nearby large city.

Services   Systems that supply the needs of the public such as police, electricity, water and transport.

Settlement   A place where people set up a community.

Site	The place where a settlement is located.
Situation	The surroundings and location of a place and how it is related to them.
Suburbanisation	The process by which outlying areas of a city are developed to provide homes for people who may travel to work in the city.
Suburbs	Outlying, mainly residential, areas of a city.
Sustainability	The management of resources so that they can be replaced and will not be used up.
Urban	Relating to a built-up environment, such as a town or a city.

FURTHER INFORMATION

People and the Planet
A website dedicated to population and environment issues with a lot of information on the growth of cities and their problems.

www.peopleandplanet.net

World cities
An Australian website about the major cities of the world.

hsc.csu.edu.au/geography/urban/cities/worldcities/World_Cities.html

Three Cities
Exploring the features of three cities at different times in history – Alexandria, Egypt 1CE; Cordoba, Spain 1000CE and New York 2000CE.

www.nationalgeographic.com/3cities/

City Population
Find out population statistics for the world's cities and locate them on the map.

www.citypopulation.de

Cities and buildings database
A growing collection of images from cities around the world.

content.lib.washington.edu/cities

Note to parents and teachers: Every effort has been made by the Publishers to ensure that these websites are suitable for children, that they are of the highest educational value, and that they contain no inappropriate or offensive material. However, because of the nature of the Internet, it is impossible to guarantee that the contents of these sites will not be altered. We strongly advise that Internet access is supervised by a responsible adult.

INDEX

INAX
MITSUKOSHI
MATSUZAKAYA
TOSHIBA
ファミリア
ロイヤルクローバー
銀座館
サンビー
LOVE